Made of Air

Made of Air

Poems by

Naomi Thiers

Cover design by Shay Culligan

ISBN: 978-1-952326-48-6

Kelsay Books
502 South 1040 East, A-119
American Fork, Utah, 84003

For Cynthia J. Estabrooks Riley (1958-2018). Early poetry friend, deft writer, and a "cathedral" who enriched my life and may once have saved it.

And, again, for Greg Luce.

So I carry these scars, so precious and rare,
and tonight I feel like I'm made of air.

—Bruce Cockburn
Northern Lights

Acknowledgments

I gratefully acknowledge the following publications in which these poems first appeared:

Broadkill Review: "Trumpet Vine," "All or None," "After Tornado Warnings," "Hidden"

Potomac Review: "Watching Susannah in the Storm"

Northern Virginia Review: "Feral"

Bourgeon: "Refugee, 15" "How Can It Be?" "Earthquake"

Kweli: "Merchant"

Yellow Arrow: "Tasmeen," "Watching You Give a Reading"

Sojourners: "Lions," "Thinking of Jairus's Daughter"

Little Patuxent Review: "All Is Calm"

Gargoyle: "Fires I Have Seen"

Deaf Poets Society: "Those Who Rise"

Oddball: "Old People Waking"

Maryland Literary Review: "How They Come Back to Us"

The following poems were included in the chapbook *She Was a Cathedral*, published by Finishing Line Press (2014): "Trumpet Vine," "Daughters Rising," "Merchant," and "Feral." "Lions" appeared in the 1992 book *Only the Raw Hands Are Heaven* (WWPH).

Contents

Ordinary Women

Remember her now—
She was a cathedral.
      —Denise Levertov

Ordinary Women

How we weave: Hidden strong arms,
and scarred, roped calves beneath swinging robes.
Skirts, robes billow as we bend, turn,
tired feet treading to the pump, the market,
to the kitchen, the courtyard, the border crossing—
like an undertow of robes and gestures,
a smoke signal of nondescript women,
children on hips or pulled pouting behind,
our bodies, even our faces unseen, eyes
on the sky.

And the walls of Jericho
shudder as in heat waves:
seen, not seen.

Lions

—It is as if lions grow inside of me, and I'm not afraid—
Mother of a "disappeared" person in Argentina

When my daughter met at night with union leaders,
I stopped talking with my neighbors.
Six strikers were found murdered,
their tongues, their hands cut from them,
and the priest said a Mass.
I pretended not to hear about it—
I begged her to stay home with me,
not to speak the names of the dead.

But when the soldiers took her
and would not give me even
the name of a prison,
the place of a grave,
I heard a roaring in my head
that swelled into my tongue, my fingers.
Now I hold up her picture in the plaza,
I call out her name,
while men with mirrors on their eyes
watch me.
I see my face reflected in their dark glass.
I do not look away.

Trumpet Vine

for Bonnie

When I think of an image
for the signature you trail
across this world,
I see a trumpet vine.

I've watched you
twist your way over cracked walls
like grace with a wire down its middle.
You turned the living rooms of gritty
houses like ours into swirling dance floors,
pulled edge lurkers, shoulders slouched over
old loneliness, into the center
to whirl in light
with you.

Your hands, vigorous
as those orange flowers,
push back despair
wherever it appears.

You brought
your brash curl of faith
into circles of boys sitting hard eyed,
in plastic chairs, 16-year-olds
who'd raped 14-year-olds.
You wouldn't shrivel: You got them

to talk, to hold up to the light
a swatch of true color,
theirs

When you say
he's withered you—
this husband who left you—I say
look how high this vine is, how many
flowers thrust bright hands
into the day.

Your Light

Somehow you spin a thread of hope, pale gold,
out of your history, your sad blood, summoning light.

You send up a flare of laughter beneath a hard load:
so many chores, sullen children. . . You drudge in light

and cup that flame even as your mood spins down
to black. Depression stalks in its studded collar. Light

a cigarette, call a friend, take your Paxil—hold on
in this season of cold mud until you sit in light

April air and smell green in the world. Brush
your long blond hair; its flood of yellow light,

its beauty, has been with you all your life,
consolation from God for the lack of light

and hope in too many days. Cherish your light.

All or None

for Carolyn

Integrity was never so buoyant
the hand of giving—and of fairness—
never so light, so angled in a joyful
invitation to dance
as with you,

friend.
It wasn't only in the swirled yellows, greens,
and ochres of your paintings—the African heat
and mysteries of your missionary childhood
that you gave your all, drenched

everyone in your vision.
It was all or nothing with you
in your cooking, your art classes, even
in your day job (the writers you edited
felt they'd been knighted), just as

you gave freely to your children—two
birthed, two adopted. When your mother
invited to visit each summer "just the two
natural ones," You said, "They're all
my children. Invite them all or none."

Carolyn,
you loved like the equatorial sun:
Rays of joy refusing
to leave anyone in shadow.

Watching Susannah in the Storm

for Lisa F.

Why does God let a mortal man have children?
It is senseless to love anything this much.

—Barbara Kingsolver

As rain rocks the earth like a judgment
you turn in your woven basket of fever.
Like a fish twisting in wicker, you do not wake
but slip past sickness and down a cool river.
I fear you, fragile, senseless one.
Since my own mother left me,
I have never poured all my love
into one vessel with a hole in the bottom.
I have kept one hand always in my pocket.

I think of my friend who watched you tonight,
held you like earth rocking its fragile spring,
seeds of mortality livening her tongue.
The changes singing in her blood may bring
her down, with all her brave luck, by the day
she's my age, and they tell me I am young.
She is the one who taught me to breathe water,
to roll along earth's crust, a wave always
arcing to break, to let fear take me deep.
To lean back, writing poems that change nothing
and listen to rain rocking my child to sleep.

Daughters Rising

My daughter pulls up, fists around her crib bars,
lips pursed firm, taking in all she sees
like Britain launching ships,
collecting continents.

I think of other daughters I have known,
women long past cradling or conquering
anything, wrapping crusty coats around themselves
at Hannah House, fingers dancing
in broken codes before their eyes.
I think of Magda in the hallway,
the skinny, piss-stained finger scratching
scabies through her boot.

Drop the light back: *Magda in a shadowed crib.*
She bears her weight, pulls up.
Her mother comes and sees her
standing, catches her up against her neck.
The flame of the small breath, the bud
of pink tongue, the smell of salt-grass hair:
no word for this but worship.

Now see her again, as half
this blistered life and half a rising daughter.
Now hold her, hold your hand
inside this flame.

Need

If I forget
to claw for the hand of God
as morning opens her mechanical wings,
raw song cawing me up into another
day, another one, come on—cold light,
linoleum, children, the gritty, inevitable
music waiting for me, the strings—

if I forget
to cradle myself awake on God's knuckle
black mornings, to rock myself slowly there,
slowly, through all my grief and need,
girding for trouble,

if I forget to plunge down the bright tunnel
tumbling toward God as if there is no hour
I will need to stop or rise, believing
infinity will hold me, have me
back in time
for my child's cries—

if I forget, I will never rise
and these mid-life fingers will age faster
than night turns to brutal dawn,
faster than sages with calculators can claim

that Jesus' grip never existed, never hauled
even one little girl out of bed
by name.

Merchant

I've glimpsed her five nights running:
a splay-footed gypsy who guards
a maroon plastic tarp draped over
mounded shopping cart, sideways
clementine crate peaking one end.
One hand rides her hip; the other elbow
leans against the greasy mound.
She looks impassively, beneath a slash
of scarf, at Beauregard Street (where
the homeless do not camp)
with the chin jut of a merchant
old in a new zone:
Here is my lot. You object?

But it is 33 degrees and pissed-off
boy-gangs roam these dull suburban streets
and white is eating through her rat-brown
hair at the temples (like mine). The sight of her
should burn, should loom,
should spur me at least
to blot her from my sight, not
to still life. I should not
complete
this transaction.

Refugee, 15

Fear is in your bread
and you must choke it down.

To think of home—
the courtyard with its red filigreed rug,
the peel-paint walls, how the breeze with its tang
of the Khabur River touched your just-cut hair
as you curled up, writing in your diary—
starts the rockslide of grief, the thundering
that blocks out sound, pulls
a knife across each breath until
you drag your body like a sack,
walking with others
toward the border.

But something rises up,
wants to live:

> *I won't be that man sitting*
> *on his burned porch, face a lace of cuts,*
> *waiting in rain for death.*

Shut away now the images of home,
like your diary with its leather straps.
Preserve your young life.
Eat your bread.

Feral

When my kid and I travel, we travel lean—
Bolt Bus, fast food, backpacks stuffed
with apples and chocolate bars—
and we trail a mild buzz: on the road again,
bouncing on Motel 6 beds.
But the day we saw her—
oh, we knew more.

At a Jerry's Subs on the edge
of Manhattan, marking time
'til the next bus, ranch sauce dripping
off subs as we leaned
on piled backpacks:

                    She sat apart
in a designer raincoat, black slacks,
her blond hair salon-waved
but pulled back in a cheap band.
Fortyish, facing hard toward the door,
chipped French manicure (I sensed
my daughter's quiet noticing), dirt stains
and bitten skin around her cuticles.

Her spine, stiff as her tower
of bags—two smart duffels
and a Filene's tote—said
Let Me Be.

She was tacking toward invisible; then
with swift, quiet movement, she rose,
walked to the corner
column of baskets,
snatched a Sun Chips
and whirled back to her perch,
one crossed leg
bouncing.
Her eyes never lifted.

She stashed the food deep
in her tote. I could see odd things
at its top (blankets, file folders),
but not her face, not her
hammering heart.

Even if
I'd had the grace to offer
an apple or drop a $20 on the floor,
her pose shut out the whole room, but—
fast as her hand stole—
my daughter's frightened
eyes shot to mine
across a full table.

For My Girl, 14, Who Writes

A backstage hand passed me something heavy
and sealed in last night's dream: an envelope
thick as the soles of the combat boots
you wear every day now, thick
as the fake-black hair curtaining your eyes.
A parcel of your heart writing, a glowing
stack, all hidden in manila.

In dream-logic, although
the flap was sealed, I could see everything
had been scrawled in eyebrow pencil,
a blunt tool meant to paint a mask,
the crayon you came to in your hurried need
to tell *and* to hide.

And I saw
how every story within would tear, would
turn to illegible smear, uncrackable
code if I pried open this package,
or riffled its pages too quickly,

as if baring to light your secrets,
your syntax, to see what's inside you
would kill this bird: your pulsing dreams,
your proud desires, even
your talent—the way you dart gleams
of golden, barbed language into every day
of low-grade talk and dead pencils.

How Can it Be?

The only way to have hope—how can it be?—
is to walk into the streets not as a beggar,
not as one crushed to a shadow, holding
a cup, begging for bread or a place to stand,
but to walk like a man in a parade, pockets
full of candy to toss to children as you pass,
as if lit from within, as if joy were
a friend you can call on any time, even

days you're too sad to dress
or untangle your hair.

Pull on
a bright shirt and walk out as if
heading to joy's house for tea and a chat.
Joy may still turn you from her door that day,
but I know hope will catch up with you, hook
her arm through yours and match your stride
even if neither of you
can speak.

Striding

for Patty Bertheaud Summerhays (1961–2009)

Chance sighting as I wait at a light:
A young woman in white jeans and strappy sandals
striding across Glebe Road, brown hair bannering.
Perhaps 23, her face just
free of child ghosts, settling
into woman, eyes set
eagerly down the road. *Blessing,*
I want to tell her, *I see broken pavement
and all-night revels ahead.*

Before the light changes
a woman in her 70s crosses behind her,
slow-moving, slim, her hair
a white crown. Black jacket,
magenta scarf; a graceful passage,
eyes no longer on fire but tipped with light.

I idle between them, struck
that at 55, I *am* between, watching
my gone youth and arriving old age
parade, and though
I seem stopped, I tick closer
to the old one every second.
                                  But not you.

Not you, dear friend. You were stopped at 48.
Frozen in mid-stride, you will never cross
with dignity to the end of a long life.

I remember your blue eyes glinting like a lake
in our 20s, remember trading our poems
and our newborns, I see you coaxing
a smile from the legless beggar in Juarez,
standing up to a coach who shamed your son.
I see you stunned, fighting, blasted by chemo.

Your shade towers in the middle of this intersection,
but for you the wheel will not turn.

Patty, I hope
that wherever you are—
for with your fierceness
I know you are somewhere—
you are striding.

Thinking of Jairus' s Daughter

for Rev. Lisa Lancaster

When I studied the book of God, I thought
I could swallow the words and become
God's page gleaming through the wilderness.

I have lived in many deserts:
the grimed brick of Pittsburgh in 1987,
its shut steel mills, its workers with spent
hands. In the hollers of Kentucky, I have prayed
over a 9-year-old with parasites.
I have tried to rub the balm of Gilead
into the side of a suburban church,
a spiteful creature that worried its own
scabs off. But I hadn't seen death swallow

its tail like this. I thought a hospital
was a calm light tunnel to life, to death,
imagined I would pour still waters,
bathe the whispery flesh of ancients.

We get the broken girlfriends from New Brunswick,
the last dignity of too many gay men
dying alone, the gang vengeances.

On call, I wake to seal the story. I'm the one
who brings the family in. Last night
someone's father was already wrapped
in plastic (nurses needing the bed).
I had to peel the clinging bag away.
I thought of Lazarus, unraveling grave clothes.
But Lord, he stinketh. What if I shut

my mind to matter, said, "I command,"
said "Lazarus, come out!" *She is not dead,*
but sleeping is a coward's
euphemism. I remember the 12-year-old
girl on a stretcher in the E.R.,
glass and blood on her naked skin,
possible paralysis. She could not hear
my voice. But I could wipe the urine

away when she wet herself in terror,
could cover her exposed breasts and trace
her body's song through her wrist. I could give
her flesh that honor—and I have come
to bow low to the flesh, to stand in awe
before the illumination of God's page.

Another Thing I Love

for my mother

Your effervescence: How
you pull stray threads of glimmer
from the brownest afternoon—
always something to laugh at.
Like the froth of petticoats brightening
the shabby courtyard of Monroeville Mall
that Wednesday—beige tiles ringing; you, Dad
and three other couples square dancing,
sweat-mooned shirts, string ties flopping
as a half-handful of people half-watched.

You were 42 then, greying, but you put
oomph into dance moves you and Dad
had learned to help heal your marriage, laughing
as you swished around a lace-sleeved dress
you'd sewn yourself.
                           Somehow,
watching this cornball show, *I* knew
a froth of pride. I understood
the gleam in your eyes
was hard-won:
my inheritance.

I Heard You Pray for Peace, Balance, and Progress

for Elizabeth

Not rivulets, not waves of food-crusted dishes,
not columns of bills and clutter on the stairway,
not three flat tires, not eight flooded cupboards,
not your son's mobius strip of questions,
not his 19th rowdy scream for attention
rattling your every other rooted tooth,
not clusters of cockroaches, not the rages, lies
the stick-to-right-angles-but-
bend-to-me demands
of your ex-demented husband,
not your mother's arched eyebrow
(on the side of said husband),
not self-doubt, not time-warps, not online predation
can stop
the motion of your progress
and the progress of your peace.

Made of Air

All Is Calm

As the winter climate unpacks, as it settles
strewing just-perceptible white dust
on newly gray hair,

there's no grimness, no suppurating wound.
All is padded, all is soft,
the grey-white world of *The Giver*.

I have misplaced some companions.

Fear, that parrot forever screeching on my shoulder,
still perches, but is stuffed
or perhaps it's flown south.

But maybe—yes, there is an ache,
the dull hurt of something near forgotten.
I miss someone:

my dancing, gnashing, dervish self.

Without the twisting of emotions, the whirlpools
How should I exist, how
feel something true in a padded world?

O, icepick of fear, cauldron of desire, even
capsaicin of humiliation,
O come back,

whirl.

Fires I Have Seen

I.

I've seen a 30-foot mushroom column of smoke
tower in a pale blue sky while I climbed
and sunned on rocks in Yosemite, slim waterfalls
glinting down cliffs, on my honeymoon.
We knew the fire was taking acres of park,
but the scale made it seem a ranger's myth
(but for that hulk of smoke and the boas
of snarling orange glimpsed on either side
of the highway in the dawn
as we evacuated, hugging, tasting
strangeness, comfort).

II.

I've seen smoke from trash fires drift through the gritty
streets of Barrio Carcamos as my "sisters"
—in Keds, Duran-Duran t-shirts, cheap belts threaded
through black jeans—snuck again out the window,
though *contra* fighters lurked in the hills down the road,
watched them flip their glossy hair as they whirled
on dirt-packed patios (always lit by
one bare bulb, with garish Christmas cards
taped to the wall for party decorations)
and weave home arm-in-arm unharmed.

III.

And I've seen a fever burn through my daughter,
consuming her before she knew words, before
I truly knew her. Months out of the womb,
face still ghosted with double brows, back
hairy from premature birth, her newly
conquering eyes drooping, forehead hot coals,
her body bursting with tubes in a crib.
Cool hands brought her back from this fire,
and in a break in the action, her round eyes
lit up, locked on mine. In that second,
I saw her interest flicker, her fragile
grip on the world surge back.

Earthquake

I can't turn around and I can't go back.
I've worn a rut in all my years of love
and worry. My life never takes me off.
I request to be reborn as a skipped rock.
I stop the car by the Bay Bridge, watch the sun—
more generous than humans are inclined to be—
cast diamonds in dirty water. That was once
my dream—to give everything I owned away.
I think of the woman driving Cypress Street Viaduct
with a van of kids who heard a god hiss: *go back.*
U-turn: working horn and chutzpah, she made it off
just before the upper deck collapsed.
I've told my kid that story, and I've dreamed
of it, the way her wheel jerked in the sun.

How They Come Back to Us

Those who have died—
their roots still spread,
their fires still spread, smoking underground.

They emerge as tree roots will, bursting out of earth
far from the hollow where we once dropped in a memory
so long ago it's only a flash, something
that once happened to a paper doll.

What comes back full color are faces,
pieces of faces: Grandma's powdered cheek,
red fuzz at Kris's temple, Patty's eye the bare-blue

of skies after rain. And there never-replaceable voices,
their vocabulary: *Sit with me once't.
How you doing there, Papa-San? I wouldn't
have that, Rosie, I just wouldn't* have *that!*

Sparks of their movements blaze—how
they danced, say: Karen's arms twirling overhead,
Kris's plant-and-stomp in Birkenstocks

Their pet ideas, coined metaphors float
in the margins as we read—as Jacklyn's motto
was suddenly there on a brick in Chincoteague:
Toujours le mot, stamped with her signature.

Like creeper vines shooting
beneath smooth lawns, bursting out to
wind around trees minding their own business

the dead still come to decorate
strange places with their unmistakable shapes,
their sudden air bracing, their unseen
heat beneath keeping us warm.

Hidden

A bridge stretched over
Four Mile Run forms a crude shelter,
a concrete pocket of unremarkable
hidden things: rusty beams, shattered
bottles, smell of dog dirt and metallic creek. Here,
where I walk every week to stretch my old body,
the ground
slopes up from the creek to the under-
side of the bridge; in that shadow
triangle where a man can't stand: three
mattresses, heaps of belongings beside them.
Nothing's
colorful here. These men, day laborers
rise at first light, roll their bedclothes,
pass quietly among us; they lose
their hometowns, their children's
photos crack and split.
Once
I glimpsed, tucked
in the shelf of a beam, a pair
of good leather work boots
enshrined, laces tied together
like silent orphans holding hands.

I stopped,
mid-stride, sucking in cold
air, felt the weight of it,
and wished:

Let them
be here when he returns, needing
boots for a three-week job, for the small
hope that comes of it: a hotel room,
a bed, a mirror, a place to shave
and in the night to bump against
his ghosts, his
hidden things.

Old People Waking

When I wake up, everything hurts. That's good. I know I'm alive.
—octogenarian interviewed by anthropologist Barbara Myerhoff

The awakening: eager, brute, or mechanical,
swinging of legs and arms to splint the body up
(from bed, sofa, woven mat)
or of hips, stubs, if the lower limbs are missing
or have gone into numbness. Nevertheless,
day breaks-up, up!

The awakening: kneading of fingers
on face, flexing the stiff upper
frame, shaking the head to the ceiling, opening
eyes still dreaming of dragon wings. Reach
for the waiting teeth, we will bite
some pleasure into this day.

It's a smaller room, a smaller life—still,
we seek the sun, we stumble to windows,
to warmth. In these naked hours, instinct
twists us toward the solar chariot,
we spent years hiding from
in gleaming towers.

And if everything hurts, it means
the current 's flowing; we hiss inside:
Live. *Live.*

Those Who Rise

Who whistle down into pill-dotted armchairs,
sofas of age-thinned textured fabric, who
lower hipbones, wince on slatted benches
or grope, frightened, with swollen ankles
for the footstool—grounded today not by fog
but by skin-splitting edema:
feet that swell, knees that grind,
fatigue that swallows all
into night-at-the-window
already, again,
another day
bound.
Who then spit, swallow panic,
push palms down on armrests, swing
titanium hips, push feet into sandals—
better today, that green tea helps—even
squint to smear plum polish,
rise up
to something.

The Pearl

At 59, I find myself reading
with the county book group the same
Steinbeck novel I studied in high school. No one
finds this strange—and stranger still, we find
passages we have to chew on.

Other evenings now, my companion
is my 20-year-old daughter.
New to her local college she has only
budding friends, so she hangs around.
Nearly two generations apart, we should have
little to say to each other—yet

it all lilts out: swapped stories
of wardrobe disasters, gossip about neighbors.
She offers manga trivia and impressions
of meaty-nosed professors, I vent
about my boss, tell my creaky tales.

As if the scald of her adolescence,
never happened, we slouch around the table
with in-jokes. I tell myself: Savor her profile,
how she tucks black commas of hair briskly

behind her ears and hums "Bohemian Rhapsody"
as she writes, fingers bouncing on her Mac

like cricket legs.
                    She's leaving soon—
                            and her rosiness too.

This cliff-high condo where we eat,
laugh and scour pots appears to me as high mesa,
a place bound by grasslands where we camp.
She can't stay here, must climb down and fight it out,

while I remain, listening to the grasses rustle,
watching rain and the sun's slide.
                              Waiting in a hang
of gentle grace tonight, I take up that book

I read when I was 16. Tracing my own
brisk marks, I taste that thick pencil I wrote with
then, breezes along the side porch where I read.
The sky and seasons inch the same as in 1976,
as if I've stood still while decades slid past,

and I savor the sense of timelessness,
this gem I never knew hid inside my bumpy life.
For I feel my own 16-year-old inside, humming
eager, terrified—real as the slow
rain of wild and gentle losses.

Watching You Give a Reading

Knowing what I know of the cracked infrastructure
beneath—the sparking of frayed wires,
beams and even foundation buckling
under their long-held burdens,
warped frames, broken circuits—
makes it sweeter
to see you stride up to a podium
speak to the gathered crowd and lift
their spirits, reset their thermostats
with the poems you chose, but also
with the bugle of your smile.
Hope
enters the room almost unnoticed
with the last straggles of audience.

I meet your eyes, blue
as any 20-year-olds.

After Tornado Warnings

Rain, banshee winds, stuttering lightening
slashed the sky all night. An hour ago,
all the drama stopped. Disasters slunk home
not having broken a single window.
When I went to take out the trash just now,
the sky was smooth and rich as an altar cloth,
the air warm, the stars high, bright, vivid
and a full moon stood above my building
white and strong as your hair, my love,
solid as your word, broad and lovely as your back.
And I stood on my steps looking up, wondering
that after all the lashing, high winds, wails of my decades
and after, really, accomplishing so little,
I was given you.

A Kind of Prayer

Still, a god's face to turn a mangled
pattern to could lift me on mornings
of white sound where a hive of cells
should be casting nets across the day, when
the message dance of my species becomes
a host of dust on my tongue: All
the wires cut and time to go to work.
Or when I know what those who know me well
would say of me after my death: little
or lies. A god's patient jerk
could redeem all this, could weave a room.

And when I write, poetry
seems no better than crocheting
afghans for The Poor, all the intricacy blurring,
the same dumb, serviceable stabbing
of hook into angora eye.
Over and over, without faith, I turn
my hand to this stabbing,
this blinded rhythm.

And though I can neither
see them nor call them,
words—like prayer—
return.

Notes

Lions: the epigraph is a quote from a Mother of the Plaza del Mayo, Argentine women whose grown children were "disappeared" by the military government in the 1970s. These mothers marched every week in protest, holding photos of their children.

Need and **Thinking of Jairus's Daughter**: See Matthew 9: 18-26

Earthquake: My parents, who experienced the 1989 Loma Prieta earthquake in San Francisco, told me this story of a woman getting off the Cypress Street Viaduct just before its collapse.

~

I'm enormously grateful to many friends and teachers who've helped me as a writer, most recently Perry Epes, Greg Luce, Miles David Moore, Jane Schapiro, & Susan Tichy.

About the Author

Naomi Thiers grew up in California and Pittsburgh, but her chosen home is in the Washington, DC area. In 1992, her poetry collection *Only the Raw Hands Are Heaven* won the Washington Writers Publishing House competition. Her other books are *In Yolo County,* and *She Was a Cathedral* (Finishing Line Press). Her poetry, fiction, and book reviews have been published in *Virginia Quarterly Review, Poet Lore, Colorado Review, Pacific Review, Potomac Review, Grist, Sojourners,* and many other magazines. Her poetry has been nominated for a Pushcart Prize and featured in anthologies, and she is a former editor of *Phoebe.* She works as an editor with *Educational Leadership* and lives in Arlington, VA, on the banks of Four Mile Run.

www.ingramcontent.com/pod-product-compliance
Lightning Source LLC
Chambersburg PA
CBHW071358090426

42738CB00012B/3163